TAMILNADU

Confrontation, Complementarity, Compromise

Israel Selvanayagam

WCC Publications, Geneva

Cover design: Edwin Hassink/WCC
Cover photo: WCC

ISBN 2-8254-1195-7

20026346

© 1996 WCC Publications, World Council of Churches,
150 route de Ferney, 1211 Geneva 2, Switzerland

No. 7 in the Gospel and Cultures series

Printed in Switzerland

TAMILNADU

Gospel and Culture pamphlets:

1. S. Wesley Ariarajah, *An Ongoing Discussion in the Ecumenical Movement*
2. Stan McKay and Janet Silman, *The First Nations of Canada*
3. Ion Bria, *Romania*
4. Noel Davies, *Wales*
5. James Massey, *Panjab*
6. Antonie Wessels, *Secularized Europe*
7. Israel Selvanayagam, *Tamilnadu*
8. Ambrose Moyo, *Zimbabwe*
9. John Pobee, *West Africa*

Table of Contents

1 1. THE CONTEXT

11 2. ASPECTS OF GOSPEL AND CULTURE

18 3. CONFRONTATION

26 4. COMPLEMENTARITY

37 5. COMPROMISE

42 6. TENSIONS AND TEMPTATIONS

54 7. TOWARDS A DIALOGICAL OPENNESS

1. The Context

Tamilnadu is a state in southeastern India, home to about 55 million people. To the east is the Bay of Bengal; its southernmost tip touches the point where the Bay of Bengal, Indian Ocean and Arabian Sea converge. Its western, northwestern and northern borders are formed by the Indian states of Kerala, Karnataka and Andhra Pradesh. Within its 130,000 square kilometres is a fantastic combination of hills and valleys, plains and seashores, well-watered fertile lands and barren areas with thorny trees. The main agricultural crop and staple food of the people is rice.

What binds the people of Tamilnadu together is Tamil, India's longest-surviving literary language. Although our focus in this pamphlet is on the interaction between gospel and culture in Tamilnadu (the name means "Tamil Country"), it should be borne in mind that approximately 800,000 Tamils occupy the neighbouring Union Territory of Pondicherry; and sizeable numbers live in the adjacent Indian states, in Sri Lanka, Malaysia and Singapore, and in Europe and the USA.

As one of the 25 states of the secular democracy of India, Tamilnadu was governed by the Congress Party for the first 20 years after independence. Since 1967, one of the sects of the Dravidian Movement has been in power, though Tamilnadu is experiencing the same politicization of religion and communalization of politics that face India as a whole. At the same time, many popular myths and stories still look back to the long history of kingdoms in this region before the establishment of British rule in the 18th century. Ideas of justice, love and charity are associated with kings.

Divisions in Tamil society

It is not easy to identify the original caste groups in Tamilnadu: the priestly class (*brahmins*), the warriors (*ksatriyas*), traders and agriculturalists (*vaisyas*) and those in servitude (*sudras*); and tremendous changes have taken place in the 19th and 20th centuries. Apart from the nomads and hill tribes belonging to different ethnic groups, it is said that the *brahmins* and *sudras* were originally predominant.

At the top are the *brahmins*, who continue to hold extraordinary power in the intellectual world, bureaucracy and religion, though a section of them have been pushed to economic backwardness. And at the bottom of the scale are those who define themselves today as Dalits, the broken ones. They have been known by a variety of other names: outcastes, exterior castes, depressed classes, scheduled castes, *harijans* ("people of God", the name Gandhi used for them). Within the Dalit community are subgroups, of which the largest is the *parayars,* the traditional drummers at Hindu ceremonies and announcers of death in the community. They are field labourers and village servants, who have been the worst victims of slavery. Somewhat higher in status are the *pallars*, the people of the valley, associated with land and agriculture. The most downtrodden are the *chakkilias* or *madharis*, who are sandal-workers, scavengers and agricultural labourers.

Between these two extremes are a large number of groups whom the *brahmins* normally consider to be sub-castes of the *sudras*, but who themselves identify with other castes in an effort to claim self-respect and social status. These include irrigators and cultivators, money-lenders, tradesmen and bankers, small-game hunters, shepherds, barbers and local physicians, carpenters, goldsmiths, stonemasons and foundry workers, accountants, writers, weavers and potters, fisherfolk living along the coast, washermen, palmyrah climbers. Some of them have undergone a process of Sanskritization, imitating the upper castes in dress and diet.

For the most part, all of these communities are spread throughout the state. Their customs and manners, way of speaking and relationships with other communities are extremely subtle and complex. Despite progressive movements calling for "one race and one people", most Tamils, even moderates, are conscious of their own caste identity;

and the deep roots of the caste system reveal themselves at times of inter-caste marriage and communal conflict.

Within this social structure, women have an ambiguous position. On the one hand, they are identified with the mother goddess and highly respected. At the same time, they are victims of perpetual oppression in both the family and society as a whole. For many men they are no more than sex objects and domestic servants. This is evident in such Tamil proverbs as "just as the tobacco leaf is disfigured when unfolded, so also the woman who laughs publicly" or "even if a piece of stone, he is a husband; and even if a blade of grass, he is a respectable partner".

Yet there are also counter-proverbs composed by women's movements and progressive thinkers; and short stories, articles and films challenge this traditional stance. It is not uncommon today to hear contradictory reports from the same place. Some justify the lower position of women in society by emphasizing the respect they enjoy in their homes. Others tell horror stories of female infanticide and foeticide, of battered women, of dowry deaths. There are now women police officers, but there are also still public nurseries for abandoned baby girls.

The basic unit of corporate living in Tamilnadu is the family. Although mobility in connection with jobs has broken up many traditional joint families, links within families are maintained in a variety of ways, including marriages within the family circle, frequent visits, taking care of parents and grandparents and bringing up children in the homes of kinsfolk.

A popular song from a Tamil film says, "The child and God are of the same character, forgetting the faults of others." Childlessness is considered unbearable, and couples will go to great lengths to have a child, particularly a son, making vows to gods and rolling around the premises of temples and shrines. A child brings special honour to its parents, particularly the mother. Yet children are among the worst victims in Tamil society. The growing number of street children is a special concern of several voluntary action groups. Movements like the Campaign Against Child Labour, founded in 1992, have uncovered heart-rending stories of the plight of working children in factories and restaurants. Estimates are that there are more than a million child labourers in Tamilnadu, working in abysmal conditions for meagre wages.

The contradictions in society are visible in all the towns and cities of Tamilnadu. To one side of the campus of the Tamilnadu Theological Seminary in Madurai, the temple town of South India and a traditional centre of Tamil culture, where I live, is the Soma Sundaram Colony, where middle- and upper-middle-class people live in a concrete jungle of houses. To the other side is the Sittalatchi Nagar slum, where rickshaw-pullers, scavengers and others live in small huts. The same phenomenon can be seen in the villages, where the large mansions in which the landlords live are surrounded by the small huts and thatched-roofed houses of the poor agricultural workers. When natural calamities and epidemics strike, many of the poor migrate to other villages or to the slums in the towns. More than half of the people of Tamilnadu live below the poverty line. Only a trickle of the resources provided by central and state government development schemes ever reach the poor; most of it is eaten up by bureaucrats. There is thus a great deal of competition within communities and petty clashes often result.

Tradition and modernity are side-by-side in the Tamil Country, often interacting in peculiar ways.

For example, primary education is compulsory except for child labourers who have to work for their daily bread. Higher education is growing; and there are eight universities in Tamilnadu and Pondicherry. In addition, there are programmes for adult literacy and education. Yet more than half the population cannot read or write. The tremendous problem of unemployment seems to diminish the enthusiasm of people for study. More significantly, one hears the question, "Who exploits the people more, the educated or the uneducated?" Corruption and red tape in administrative offices, including those of educational institutions, cause untold misery and hardship for common people. Education without enlightenment and knowledge without commitment have proved to be an unhealthy if not disastrous mix.

The judiciary is well structured, with a high court in Madras and district courts in all the districts and magistrates in small towns. But in some areas traditional village courts are still popular and disputes are settled by respected elders and leaders.

Public and private hospitals are found in all the cities and towns and in a growing number of rural areas. But many people continue to use the traditional country medicines made of herbs and other natural articles; and the Tamil *siddha* medication is now approved by the government. Contradictions prevail in the world of health care. The sanitary conditions in the large government hospitals are very poor; and although modern medical equipment is available there, the poor and illiterate masses have scarcely any access to it. The decorative ambulance serve is not matched by a public health service.

The technological advances evident in the factories in the towns have not eased the lot of the *beedi* workers and those in the cashew-nut factories who must still work with their hands. Landlords and large farmers use motorized tractors and irrigation pumps, while the small farmers still till their fields with traditional ploughshares pulled by bullocks.

In addition to the huge international and domestic airport in Madras, towns like Tiruchirappalli, Coimbatore and Madurai are connected by domestic airlines. The number of trains, buses, cars and motorized two- and three-wheeled vehicles is growing; and it is not uncommon to see the latest model automobiles making their way along the muddy roads near paddy fields. But on the highways and byways they must overtake bullock carts and in the narrow streets of the villages they compete with bicycles.

In the area of communication, Tamilnadu is one of India's leading producers of books, daily newspapers and magazines. But all of this is out of reach of millions of people, though there are also newspapers for those who cannot read. Every major town has a regional station of All India Radio. Many villages have public radio receivers; and for most rural folk, a radio is the top item on the list of luxuries to acquire when they are able. Television, recently introduced, is increasingly popular. But in the slums and villages the most effective and popular medium for informa-tion-sharing continues to be gossip in the community.

Oral traditions preserved in memory are transmitted to the younger generation, but the popularity of cinema has led to the decline of traditional folk dances and dramas, though some groups are working hard to revive these. Street theatre is a novel form that has come to be used to mobilize people's awareness of social problems. Similarly, the modern sports world has seemed to swallow up the simple and traditional local games. In villages I have seen boys playing cricket using ordinary sticks for bats and stumps, a rubber ball and a piece of sack cloth around their knees.

In all of these areas, the common factor is that the "gifts of modernity" are enjoyed by only those who have some economic security and are on the higher rungs of the social ladder. While many manage to ignore the plight of those on the lower rungs or even crawling on the ground for survival by portraying this in terms of the "plurality and multiplicity of the Tamil context", a few people have begun to speak out about the sheer contradictions in all this.

Culture and religion

Tamil has a long and rich literary heritage. The ancient Tamil poems called the Sankam literature, which probably began to emerge about two thousand years ago, remain the pride of the Tamil tradition. This consists of eight anthologies (*Ettuthokai*), ten songs (*Patthuppattu*), an ancient grammar (*Tolkappiam*) and eighteen shorter texts

(*Pathinen Kilkanakku*) by no fewer than 473 authors. They seem to have a common tone and spirit, and with sophisticated symbolic conventions they achieve considerable richness and depth of language within the confines of simple, straightforward lyric poetry.

The Sankam poetry has two parts, inner (*akam*), dealing with love and passion, and outer (*puram*), dealing with ethical notions, community and kingdom. Its vivid descriptions of the natural features of the Tamil countryside are often referred to in writing and speaking. In the interior poetry, the landscape is divided into five well-defined regions, each named for its most characteristic flower: *kurinchi* (hills), *mullai* (forest and pastureland), *marutham* (agricultural fields), *neithal* (seacoast) and *palai* (desert). The typical characteristics of each region are associated with its fauna, flora and particular deities and with different moods of the lovers.

The foremost work of the *Pathinen Kilkanakku* are 1330 sacred couplets (*Tirukkural*) of Tiruvalluvar, which is called the "scripture of the Tamils". The poet, who seems to have been influenced by Jainism (though the couplets are generously quoted by all religious groups) speaks of the four goals of human life as defined by the brahmanic tradition: moral order (*aram* or *dharma*), wealth (*porul* or *artha*), love and passion (*inbam* or *kama*) and liberation (*vidu* or *moksha*). All over Tamilnadu travellers will find these couplets written on public walls and the backs of seats in the buses.

Following the Sankam literature and before the rise of devotional poetry in the 7th century, the five major Tamil epics arose. These epics, which extol the virtues of justice and renunciation, bear the marks of an increasing Aryanization of Tamil literature and religion and the influence of Buddhism and Jainism.

Of the Tamil devotional texts from the Vaishnava Hindu community, the most important is the collection of 4000 verses (*Nalayira Divyaprabhandham*) composed by the twelve *Alvars*, who perished in the divine love of Vishnu.

The parallel scriptures from the Saiva Hindu tradition are the twelve canonical texts of which the most famous is the sacred utterance (*Tiruvacakam*) of the poet-saint Manikkavacakar, describing the supremacy and intimacy of Lord Siva. These were followed by the fourteen philosophical texts of Saiva Siddhanta, which were produced around the 12th century.

In addition, there are numerous devotional poems and local legends recited by people on important occasions. And the production of devotional literature continues.

The Aryanization of Tamil literature and religion is a complex historical process and most opinions remain at the level of conjecture. Some scholars have found a few references in the Sankam literature to Siva or his prototype, the Supreme Being of the Tamil Saivites. There are also a few references to the Vedic gods Vishnu (Mayon), Indra and Varuna. But Murugan and Kottavai stand out as the traditional Tamil god and goddess. Murugan was later identified with Siva's son Skanda, his brother being the elephant-headed Ganesh (Vinayaka or Pillaiyar). Kottavai is a ferocious goddess who demanded gruesome sacrifices. Later she was identified with Durga and other goddesses, who are taken as different manifestations of the supreme power (*Sakti*).

The Vaishnavas and Saivites are the two major Hindu communities in Tamilnadu, with temples all over the state. The Vaishnava tradition gives prominence to the Sanskrit language, Vedic ritual and brahmanic priesthood. Vaishnava priests are called Iyenkars. Vishnu's two *avatars* or descending forms, Rama and Krishna, are popular among the Tamils. The *Kamba Ramayanam* is a Tamil version of the epic *Ramayana*, depicting the story with Tamil features. The favourite Tamil name for Krishna is Kannan ("one who has eyes"). There are a few translations of and commentaries on the Bhagavad Gita in Tamil. Since the Tamil tradition is part of the southern school, in which the analogy for divine grace and human response is the cat and kitten (over against the northern school's analogy of the monkey and her children), undeserved grace is acknowledged in the devotional texts with an outpouring of devotion to Vishnu and a sense of absolute surrender.

The Tamil Saiva tradition is less brahmanic, as it has incorporated more local traditions into its framework, although the brahmin priesthood is tightly safeguarded in the major temples. The Saiva brahmin priests are called Iyers. Several goddesses from earlier Tamil cults are taken as different forms of Siva's consort. There are separate shrines for Murugan and Pillaiyar, the two sons of Siva, while Mari is the most popular goddess with independent shrines. Vedic ritual, puranic stories and local legends together contribute to the complexity of the Tamil Saiva tradition. Most prominent is the emphasis on love and devotion.

The basic problem recognized in both the Vaishnava and Saiva traditions is the bondage of the soul to the chain of births, with the effect of suffering due to accumulated actions performed in previous lives. Devotees sing that Vishnu or Siva can break this chain and remove the bondage through his grace and love, promising a life of liberation, joy and permanence in close intimacy with God.

There have been moments of conflict between the Vaishnava and Saiva traditions, but also ecumenical attempts to bring them together, including the Iyyappa cult, which has a large number of devotees in Tamilnadu.

Apart from these traditions closely associated with classical brahmanism, there are diverse cults and folk traditions. While some scholars argue that these are in fact the original indigenous Tamil traditions unaffected by Aryanization, the ambiguous beliefs and practices of their devotees, who also make pilgrimages to Vaishnava or Saiva temples, make it difficult to ascertain this. Contemporary Hindu revivalist movements have sought to bring all cultic traditions under one umbrella.

Cave-temples and other monuments suggest that there were once Buddhists and Jains in Tamilnadu. According to historians, the rise of the Saiva and Vaishnava devotional movements crushed their influence, causing many of their devotees to flee, and today there are only small groups of Buddhists and Jains, who do not give much outward expression to their religion.

Muslims make up a formidable minority of about 10 percent of the population of Tamilnadu. Despite their religious distinctiveness, they have contributed considerably to Tamil literature and culture. Remarkably, they in turn have incorporated elements of Tamil religious ideas and practices into their traditions. There are a few festivals peculiar to local Muslims; and *darga* (tombs of the saints) worship, devotional singing and miraculous healing are popular.

A little over 6 percent of the population are Christians, with approximately equal numbers of Catholics and Protestants. The main Protestant churches include the Church of South India (formed in 1947 by the union of Anglicans, British Methodists, Presbyterians and Congregationalists) and several Lutheran churches. Numerous worldwide charismatic churches and groups have branches in Tamilnadu, and sectarian groups and individual preachers with private establishments add to the complexity of the Christian panorama.

Christians are well-recognized in Tamilnadu through their regular worship (in church buildings which remind others of their Western origins) and their medical and educational institutions. The enthusiasm of some Christians in propagating the Christian message is generally tolerated if done modestly, but arouses vigorous reactions if it is fanatical and irritating.

In the survey in the remainder of this pamphlet we will have more to say about both the Christian presence in Tamilnadu and many of the aspects of Tamil culture outlined very sketchily above.

2. Aspects of Gospel and Culture

Although the terms "gospel" and "culture" both elude fully satisfactory definition, it may be helpful to begin our treatment by drawing from the Tamil context to illustrate some of the essential and fundamental elements of gospel and culture.

Understanding gospel and culture

Gospel is essentially the liberating power of God, which is communicated in words and demonstrated in actions. This liberating power touches all dimensions of life, guiding it to a stage of perfection, of which Jesus was the supreme symbol. He asked people to follow him and told them, "Be perfect, therefore, as your heavenly Father is perfect" (Matt. 5:48). The context of this saying is a description of how God in fact deals with humanity, making the sun to rise on the evil as well as the good and sending rain on both the just and the unjust.

The basic attitude implied in this description is the ability to love the unlovable. Inevitably, this involves suffering; and the followers of Jesus find the suffering love of God manifested in the suffering of Jesus and his death on the cross. This love can be resisted, but it cannot be destroyed. By raising Jesus from the dead, God set forth hope for all humanity. God continues to call all people through his Spirit and calls his servants to respond to this love by reorienting their lives on a foundation of love, reconciliation, justice and peace and by working for the transformation of all aspects of life in society and in the world. In this respect, the potential for liberation found in other persons and traditions are theologically significant for the Christian gospel as well.

Culture covers all aspects of human life, both individually and in community, ranging from the way people hum or whistle or raise their eyebrows to the pattern of their dress and food to the ways in which they think and communicate with each other. Thus the aspects of culture do not emerge when we talk about it as an abstract concept but rather when

12

we narrate the stories and experiences of people in their particular context.

A fundamental aspect of Tamil culture is its holistic vision of life, weaving together awareness of the divine, relationships with nature and feelings for one's fellow human beings in an amazing variety of shifting combinations. The devotional literature of both the Saiva and Vaishnava traditions reflects this holistic vision to only a small degree, since the fundamental problem it deals with is the search for liberation from the chain of births; but the deities of these traditions share this vision to a greater extent.

The Sankam literature does not make a dichotomy between religion and secular life. The gods and goddesses are involved in human affairs and associated with the beauty of nature and with passion in human relationships. The ancient Tamils experienced a kind of immanent, impersonal sacred power inherent particularly in women and kings. For a man to touch a woman outside of wedlock was seen as dangerous, but at the wedding this power was converted into something benevolent. If the parents of a man's beloved resisted his wish to marry her, he would ride through the streets on a thorny cart with bleeding wounds; and the society would not tolerate their continued resistance.

The sacred couplets (*Tirukkural*) speak of various themes like practical education, modesty of women, proper use of wealth, respect for parents and love. One couplet compares a loveless person to a body without bones. Charity and hospitality are highly praised, and a sense of justice seems to be embedded in the people's unconscious. Thus a common lamentation when shocked by an event is "What an injustice!"

Pongal, which takes place in the middle of January, is considered the major festival of the Tamils. It involves cooking raw rice in a decorated new mud-pot without draining the water. The spilling over of the rice and water are seen as signifying the fullness of life. The celebrations also include the decorating of cows, the sharing of sugar cane or sweet rice and the heroic sport of fighting with giant bulls.

A pilgrimage of understanding

Even the brief sketch in the previous chapter of the major Tamil religious traditions has given a hint of their richness and complexity. Moving away from one's own village to another place in Tamilnadu is also a journey of learning about new cults and practices. Let me illustrate this with a brief account of my own ongoing pilgrimage of understanding Hinduism. [1]

"Don't cross, go around!", I remember my father sometimes telling me as we walked together along an untracked way on the outskirts of our village of Parakkanvilai in Kanyakumari District of Tamilnadu, one kilometre inland from the Indian Ocean. "Some people have sacrificed to a ghost here, and if we step on the remnants we will have trouble."

Only later, when I had studied Hindu belief, did I come to understand something of how ghosts operated in the minds of our neighbours. The ghosts, whose names pointed to their place of origin (usually a jungle or a hill), were either inherited by a family from its ancestors or brought from another village under certain conditions. There are popular stories about ghosts wandering around in the form of a very tall figure who does not touch the ground, an attractive woman or a black dog.

The basic terms of the relationship were that the owner would make regular blood sacrifices to the ghost and the ghost would rescue the owner from trouble and exact vengeance on his enemies. If there was any doubt about the ghost's operations, the owner would perform a special sacrifice and ask the ghost questions at the sacrificial spot. Magicians and wandering shamans are available to recommend or prescribe such sacrifices.

The most common form of sacrifice was very simple: plant four Indian coral tree poles and hang tender palm leaves and a basket from them. Kill a rooster, sprinkle the blood on the poles and put the flesh in the basket. Cook the meat and eat it with newly boiled rice, adding things like bananas if one wishes. Sometimes such sacrifices would take place in the central hall of the house; and the poles, leaves and basket would remain in place for a long time.

At the centre of all ritual activities is a clay effigy of the ghost, lying down with a terrifying look on its face. I remember the horror I felt at the sight of this figure — once in my own village at the home of my friend Pauldhas, once in a nearby village at the home of my sister, who had married a Hindu. In each case, the family had gone through a series of misfortunes, and had made the sacrifice in order to find a remedy.

There are other cults in Parakkanvilai as well. Shaded by a large tree on the northern edge of the village, a small open shrine with a stone image of two cobras is maintained by a community called *kuruppu*, a subcaste of the traditional *sudras*, who are considered higher than the majority of the village, the *nadars*, whose traditional occupation was palmyrah-tapping and who were once considered untouchable. On various auspicious occasions, marked by bursting firecrackers and concerts, people gather here. In November and December, the devotees of Ayyapa, an increasingly popular deity whose main shrine is in Kerala, come here to chant prayers. The accompanying concerts and other functions, sometimes with the offer of free porridge, are attended by people of all communities and religions.

At the other end of the village are two shrines overshadowed by bunyan trees, one for the ferocious Kali and the other for her sister Isakki. These goddesses are said to be benevolent to some of their devotees, meeting them in mysterious ways and blessing them. The two shrines are managed by the *nadar* community. The most memorable annual event here is a three-day festival, culminating in the frenzied running of a palmyrah-tapper possessed by the goddesses, who takes boiling water with a bunch of coconut flowers and sprinkles it on his body.

In the middle of the village is a shrine managed by a few families in which there is a clay statue of the goddess Isakki standing with a baby at her left ankle. Occasional functions of the kind mentioned above, though on a smaller scale, are held here.

Just opposite it is the Christian church in the village, now a congregation of the Church of South India. It was founded by missionaries of the London Missionary Society (LMS) in the 19th century, when masses of people, mainly *nadars*, became Christians. This church has grown steadily through new converts.

It is interesting that the Christians in Parakkanvilai are called *Vedakkarar* ("people of the *Veda*", a term adapted from Hinduism to denote the Bible) and the Hindus *annanis* ("people of ignorance"). Yet there has been no conflict between Hindus and Christians here, and socially they live together with many common bonds. There may be criticism of each other in conversations, but it takes place in fun and laughter. Even a radical conversion from the Hindu community does not create any great stir. When my friend Martin Selvam became a Christian through the work of the youth gospel fellowship of the church, he denounced his family ghosts and broke his family shrine and the icon. Now he is an active member of the local church, having brought many more from his family. The same youth fellowship motivated me to take up pastoral ministry and kept a close association with me during my four years of probation in a village congregation some 15 kilometres away.

When I became a student at Tamilnadu Theological Seminary in Madurai in 1973, I discovered many things that were strange to me. The high liturgical traditions of the Lutheran and Anglican churches were far different from the simple free-form worship of my own congregational tradi- tion, as were the experiments going on with indigenous forms of worship. Adding to the bewilderment was the atmosphere of Madurai itself, with its hundreds of temples and wayside shrines in addition to the famous temple of the fish-eyed goddess Meenakshi. The seminary as a whole was struggling to adapt to this context, for it had been established in Madurai only four years earlier by a merger of two seminaries which had been situated in exclusively Christian ghettoes: one in Tranquebar, the Lutheran headquarters, the other in Tirumaraiyoor, near Nazareth, a high Anglican centre. The principal and several of the teachers made the theological community constantly aware of the resources and challenges of Madurai, which is the centre of the Tamil Saiva tradition and Tamil culture and language. It was common to meet Hindus on the campus, not only reading in the library but also as visiting lecturers and part-time music teachers.

Although I had heard the terms *Veda* and *Bhagavad Gita* before coming to Madurai, I had no idea whatever of their nature or teaching. So when I studied Hinduism as part of the course on major religious traditions of India, I felt I was being introduced to an entirely new world. Through the Religious Friends Circle of the seminary I met a variety of Hindus, ranging from worshippers at wayside shrines in the city to the devotees of Satya Sai Baba, a popular modern guru and wonder-worker who is regarded as one of the incarnations of God.

Later, my advanced studies of Hinduism, especially my research in *Tiruvacakam* and Vedic sacrifice, made me more aware of the complex and multifarious religious traditions of Tamilnadu. An important consequence of this was that I no longer think of gospel and Tamil culture in the singular, but try to take seriously the particular aspects of the culture of the person of a particular religious tradition I encounter and relate the particular dimensions of the gospel which I find relevant, although there are of course also occasions for discussing the fundamental framework or core vision of my faith and that of others.

The next three chapters reflect on gospel and culture in the Tamil context under three headings: confrontation, complementarity and compromise. This is followed by a chapter on some of the tensions and temptations in linking gospel and culture, then a concluding chapter pleading for a stance of "dialogical openness".

NOTE

[1] The following is adapted from the first chapter of my book *The Dynamics of Hindu Traditions: Teape Lectures on Gita, Sacrifice and Dialogue*, Bangalore, Asian Trading Corporation, 1995.

3. Confrontation

To speak of the gospel confronting Tamil culture is not to suggest that at one moment it attacked a single system, but rather that it affected aspects of it, directly and indirectly, through a long process. This can be illustrated by a number of episodes from the history of Christian mission in this area.

Mission history

According to tradition, the earliest encounter of gospel and culture in South India goes back to apostolic times. St Thomas Mount and San Thome Church in Madras are monuments to the ministry and death of St Thomas, one of Jesus' disciples, who is said to have come to Kerala in the first century to establish churches. When he preached in Madras, his message so disturbed the hegemony of the brahmins that a group of them killed him. Those Christians today who emphasize that the gospel must be anti-brahmanic find a model in the story of this first evangelist to Tamilnadu, confronting a longstanding system of oppression and as a result being the victim of a gruesome murder.

In the middle of the 16th century, when the Portuguese had firmly established themselves on the west coast, the Spanish Jesuit St Francis Xavier (1506-52) made several journeys to India. During one of them he converted the fisherfolk on the east coast to Christianity. These fisherfolk were considered abominable by those who lived inland; to this day, although most of the coastal villagers are Catholics, the people of the inland, even their fellow-Christians, have no social contact with them. When unscrupulous colonists and local kings oppressed and persecuted the fisherfolk, Francis Xavier took advantage of Portuguese patronage to help them. The people of these areas remain attached to the Christian gospel, because Francis Xavier treated them as humans — a vivid example of making a people out of what was "no people" (cf. Hos. 2:23).

Similar situations of misery and oppression from several centuries later are vividly depicted in historical documents regarding the plight of the *shanar* or *nadar* community in

Kanyakumari District, which was previously part of the Kingdom of South Travancore. [1] Society here was based on an hierarchical caste system, and slavery was officially recognized until the mid-19th century. Numerous acts of inhuman cruelty were meted out to low-caste slaves by their high-caste masters. One account tells the story of Madathy, a slave living in the village of Thazhakudi:

> She was in an advanced state of pregnancy; starved, sick and weak, she could hardly move around. Naked, starving children with matted hair and filthy clothes tugged at her for food as she lay crumpled on the floor in the corner of her hovel between fatigue and semi-consciousness. There would be no food in the house till the evening, when her husband, who had gone out to work in the master's field, would bring his scanty earnings.
>
> That was an auspicious day for ploughing the rice-fields, and the landlord had ordered all his slaves, men and women, to come for work in the morning. Madathy knew that failure to report would entail severe punishment, but she was too ill to care. She heard the sound of approaching steps. Yes, these were men, slaves like her, sent by the landlord to take her to the field, if necessary by force. Her remonstrances were of no avail. She dragged herself to the field, where the landlord ordered her to be yoked to a plough along with a buffalo and to pull the plough, to the utter horror of everyone. This resulted in her death. [2]

Another gross denial of rights was the restrictions which the strict conventions of the caste system placed on the dress of lower-caste women:

> They were bidden to wear a coarse piece of cloth known as *mundu*, extending from the waist to the knees, leaving the breasts bare. A woman was given one or two *mundus* a year by her master. Working in the fields from morning till evening, standing knee-deep in water in the rain and the sun, planting and weeding, wearing the same piece of cloth day in and day out, with hardly the facility or the time to wash, they went about in filthy rags, foul-smelling and really "untouchable". Like dumb driven cattle, these poor women accepted

the mandates of the higher castes who denied their human-hood.[3]

Seeing the sufferings of these women, Ringletaube, the first Christian missionary to this district, made representations to the colonial authorities, who helped to free them from the poll-tax and from service on Sunday in the Hindu temples and granted permission for the women "to cover their bosoms as obtained among Christian women in other countries". But although a government order in May 1814 allowed *nadar* women converts to Christianity to wear jackets (*kuppayam*) as worn by Syrian Christians and others, the higher castes continued to block these concessions.[4]

Along with this "Upper Cloth Movement" and efforts to abolish the poll-tax, the missionaries started lace industries for women to make their own garments, opened hospitals and founded schools and colleges, including schools for the blind, deaf and mute. But even today people of this area are paying the price for this great transformation "from ignominy to disunity"; and there have been recent incidents of communal clashes touched off when caste Hindus have instigated *nadar* Hindus to take vengeance against Christians.

Liberation in Tirunelveli

In Tirunelveli, to the north, the liberation of women and of outcaste *nadars* and *shanars* was also the outcome of the work of those who sought to transform society through the gospel. Clarinda, the widow of a Marathi *brahmin* employed by the king of Tanjavur and a person of great intellectual vigour, was the first woman leader of the budding Christian community:

Many were the keen contests, theological and dialectical, which took place in her house between the adherents of the Roman Catholic and the Protestant faiths, and she was a clever and able exponent of the latter. Even conversions from the older to the later dogma are recorded, presumably following these discussions. Two families of *shanars* who lived in one of the several villages which she held in mortgage — Terivilai, to the south of Palamcottah — became Christians and are said to have been "the firstlings of that caste". She preached the gospel to her Hindu countrymen and countrywomen in her own house, and her "exhortations often produced a good effect". In order to help her in the work, she appointed a catechist, Maria Savari, at her own cost. Her charities increased...

With the growing success of her labours in the cause of Christianity, the absence of a Protestant church in Palamcottah, which had a considerable congregation, native and European, troubled her mind; and in the year 1783 she conceived the idea of supplying the desideratum at her own expense... She built a small chapel, which exists to this day, and which was the first Protestant church in what is now numerically the greatest Christian district in all India.[5]

The rapid establishment of churches in Tirunelveli District was a major breakthrough in a caste-ridden society, as the Christian fellowships provided a sense of community. Christians proclaimed, sometimes in an exaggerated way, that they were liberated from social depression, fate and demons. They spoke out boldly and sang joyfully of the liberating power of Jesus. A special concentration on education made Madurai a centre for Christian groups from Tirunelveli and elsewhere. Christian schools and colleges have attracted not only pupils from the surrounding villages but also local Hindus and Muslims. Educational institutions have also been established in neighbouring areas, particularly in Ramanathapuram District, a remote, dry and backward area where the slogan "Opening the eyes of Tamils through education" is especially fitting.

Opposition to slavery and medical mission

The missionaries' spirit of service and their concern for people, especially those oppressed by the caste structure, were expressed in many different ways. Various types of bonded labour and slavery — hereditary, penal, domestic — have existed throughout Tamilnadu since at least the early mediaeval period; and the tyranny of this system, whose ally was untouchability, has been abundantly documented. A Tamil historian has reflected on the effect of the efforts by early missionaries in Tanjavur, Tiruchirappalli, Chengalpattu and South Arcot "to fight famine and unemployment, to control epidemics, to found schools and hospitals and to run orphanages":

> By providing education and medical aid to the *harijans*, orphans, women, lepers and tribal people — the people whose need was greatest — the missionaries have made a real contribution to Indian society.
>
> Missionary agitation for the vindication of the legal rights of the outcaste people was equally great. By the power of their tongue and the might of their pen they stimulated public discussion on the wrongs done to this community from which were drawn the largest number of bonded slaves. By sending deputations and presenting memorandums to the government, the missionary societies moved the official world to redress the social evils and injustices done to the *harijans* through legislation...
>
> The missionaries lost no time in launching a vigorous attack on certain Hindu practices such as untouchability, the degraded position of women, child marriage and polygamy and bonded labour. They severely criticized the practice of caste, which is the source of division and misfortune. They actively opposed it, for in the first place, the Christian church could not exist in caste with her sacraments, and secondly, the idea of equality implicit in the Christian gospel is of such revolutionary character that it sharply contradicts the Hindu idea of spiritual hierarchy implicit in caste. [6]

Slavery still continues in different forms, though it is weakened considerably. The government claims that the system of bonded labour is abolished, but there are action groups, including a few Christian ones, which have identified bonded labourers in certain pockets of Tamilnadu and are working for their emancipation.

We have earlier mentioned the medical work which is part of the Christian mission all over Tamilnadu but nowhere with a higher profile than at the famous Christian Medical College and hospital in Vellore, one of the most noteworthy medical centres in all of Asia. A picturesque description of the contrasts found at the hospital is recorded in a biography of its founder:

> Young Indian doctors in crisp uniforms, moving with the same brisk efficiency as their counterparts in Johns Hopkins or the Mayo Clinic. Patriarchs in long skirts and flowing shirts topped by skullcap or fez or turban. Holy men with Vishnu's trident or the three bars of Shiva scored in sandalwood paste on their foreheads. Student nurses in blue-and-white saris. Officials looking equally impressive in Western suit or Gandhi cap and *vaishti*. Villagers wearing only a strip of cloth about head and loins, yet possessing the peculiar dignity that is endowed by centuries of burden-bearing. Women with smooth braids and silken saris, glowing with the excitement of a newly discovered independence. Women still peering timidly from the ancient folds of purdah veils. Women with patient eyes and hard bare feet. Children clean and dirty, dressed and undressed, laughing, whimpering, crying, faces bright with health and pinched with misery. [7]

Ida Scudder came to Vellore in 1878 and worked for fifty years as a medical missionary of the American Arcot Mission. She and doctors like her were sources of inspiration to millions of Tamil women to come out of their homes, study and minister to the sick people in various ways. Even today, wherever serious discussion about mission and the power of the gospel takes place, healing is a central point of concern.

Different perspectives on confrontation

We have mentioned at several points the ambiguous beliefs and practices of people belonging to the folk traditions of Tamilnadu. Some Christians would not hesitate to say that the word "ambiguous" in this sentence should be replaced by the word "superstitious". Without entering into this debate here, it must be acknowledged that it remains a knotty question how one should look at such common sights

24

in Madurai and other villages of towns as people rolling around the premises of temples and shrines, shaving their heads, inflicting wounds on their bodies, making and fulfilling vows, consulting shamans, astrologers and horoscopes, walking on fire, being filled with evil spirits or the spirits of their deities, worshipping at trees or anthills, revering snakes, making idols, practising blood sacrifice. Some Hindu reformers have condemned these and similar practices as lower forms of religion. Hindu revivalists seem to justify them, offering "scientific explanations". But those who take Jesus as the greatest critic of religion and who see the gospel as the highest form of religion denounce them, some mildly, some boldly.

One final observation. To a great extent, the social and economic liberation of people in different parts of Tamilnadu initiated and promoted by the early missionaries enjoyed the support of the colonial rulers, especially the British. Today, all this is seen from different points of view. For some, the compassion and humanitarianism of the white missionaries marks them as helping angels. For others, they seem to have been demons who were only supporting the oppression and economic exploitation of their rulers. Naturally, there are some who try to take a middle position, recognizing both the tensions and dilemmas in this mission work, reflecting the typical attitude of Tamils towards the British rulers and their officials.

NOTES

[1] This account is based on Joy Gnanadason, *A Forgotten History: The Story of the Missionary Movement and Liberation of People in South Travancore*, Madras, Gurukul Lutheran Theological College and Research Institute, 1994.
[2] *Ibid.*, pp.17f.
[3] *Ibid.*, p.35.

4. Complementarity

To speak of the complementarity of gospel and culture implies that resources are available within the culture which can be used to communicate the gospel. What points of contact are present for interpreting and even enriching the message of the gospel by incorporating newer elements? What indirect influence might the gospel have on a renaissance of certain aspects of the culture?

Some stories from mission history

Does the gospel appeal only to the outcaste and the poor or is there a way of approaching high-caste people with it? This question was raised by Robert De Nobili, a young Jesuit missionary who came to Madurai in 1605. He decided to adopt the life-style of a brahmanic monk. Mastering the Sanskrit language, which was regarded as sacred and had an influence on Tamil, he studied the Vedas and the philosophical traditions of brahmanic Hinduism. De Nobili wanted to train future Indian Christian priests in a way that would enable them to present the gospel in the language and thought-forms of their people. He asked permission from Rome to substitute Sanskrit for Latin in the liturgy. He composed a *Life of Our Lady* in verse and wrote a summary of Christian doctrine in one hundred Sanskrit verses. De Nobili also wrote books in Tamil, including a catechism.

Although De Nobili's attitude to Hinduism was entirely negative, denouncing particularly the doctrines of rebirth and *avatar*, he evolved a Christian theological vocabulary for Indian languages, interpreted the Bible as the fifth Veda and ate vegetarian food, thus laying the foundation for later Indian Catholic attempts at inculturation.

Joseph Constantius Beschi (1680-1747) was an Italian missionary who came to Tamilnadu in 1711. His mastery of Tamil was such that he wrote three books in Latin on Tamil grammar. Beschi compiled Tamil-Latin and Portuguese-Tamil-Latin dictionaries. His dictionary of Tamil in Tamil laid the foundation for later lexicographical works; and even today Tamil scholars gratefully acknowledge his important contributions to the language. His most famous work was an epic on the life of Joseph, incorporating ideas and idioms from the Tamil epics and other poetry and portraying Mary as a Tamil woman. Such daring explorations into the Tamil world led him to describe himself as *Thairiyanatha Swamy* ("courageous monk").

The first Protestant missionary to India was Bartholomäus Ziegenbalg, who landed at Tranquebar on the east coast of Tamilnadu in 1706. Ziegenbalg, a member of the German pietist group in Halle, arrived determined to convert the Tamils, but he was surprised by the devotion and moral quality of several Hindus whom he met. Consequently, even before completing a translation of the New Testament into Tamil, he made an extensive study of Hindu beliefs, visiting shrines and collecting information. He wrote up his findings in a manuscript which he sent back to Germany, but the director of the Halle mission replied that publishing it would be unthinkable, since "the missionaries were sent out to extirpate heathenism, and not to spread heathenish nonsense in Europe". The manuscript was put on a shelf for more than a century-and-a-half before it was finally published.

In fact, Ziegenbalg himself used the terms "foolish" and "blind" to describe what he called the "heathenism" of the Tamils. Yet referring to the popular Hindu belief in one supreme almighty God, he wondered

> how much further they have of his knowledge by the light of nature than the heathens of Rome. But the light of nature has been quite obscured by their ancient poets and Brahmins, who have written many fabulous stories and introduced a confused idol worship, out of which they cannot easily extricate themselves, though they feel much opposition to it in their conscience and can speak very reasonably of the Supreme Being. [1]

At one point Ziegenbalg speaks of God "as the object of Christian faith and the subject of Hindu speculation". [2] His pioneering reflections on Hinduism had a far-reaching influence on the attempts of certain later missionaries.

Among the black statues erected by the government along the Marina Beach in Madras is one of an Anglican bishop of Tirunelveli, Robert Caldwell (1819-1891), who contributed to the growth of Tamil self-consciousness by demonstrating that the Tamil language is distinct from Sanskrit and is in fact the root of all the major South Indian languages. He wrote a monumental *Comparative Grammar of the Dravidian or South Indian Family of Languages* (1875); and it was indeed he who gave to these languages the name "Dravida", which is probably a Sanskrit corruption of the term "Tamil". Later social and political movements used this name in the interest of the renaissance of Tamil identity. In fact, whether the Dravidians were racially Aryan or were an originally "Scythian" group who came to India before the Aryans remains a matter of scholarly dispute. The term is also reflected in *Adidravida*, a word that Dalits or outcastes use to identify themselves as the indigenous people of the soil.

Buried in a tomb in Oxford that bears the inscription "A Tamil Student" is G.U. Pope (1820-1907), a missionary of the Society for the Propagation of the Gospel who worked in Tirunelveli. To him goes the credit for the first translation of the famous Tamil Saiva text *Tiruvacakam* into English, published by the Oxford University Press in 1900. Pope's notes on the text and his introduction to Saiva Siddhanta are still highly valued. It is said that Pope was in tears when he was translating this text, with its unique appeal of overflowing devotion and poetic nuance, which he compared to the Psalms of David. In addition he translated *Naladiyar* and *Tirukkural*, thus introducing the English-speaking world to the rich ethical resources in the Tamil tradition.

Tamil Christian poets

Of the Christian poets converted from Hinduism who still drank from the wells of Tamil devotional poetry, the most famous and influential in Tamil Christian circles are Vedanayagam Sastriyar (1774-1864) and Henry Alfred Krishnapillai (1827-1900). Their lyrics continue to be sung in worship and their writings are studied in schools. Their conversion experience is celebrated and many Christians seem to follow literally and in spirit their way of looking at their old religions.

Both Sastriyar and Krishnapillai belonged to the *Vellalar* community, one of the highest non-Brahmin castes, and both came from Tirunelveli, where the Church Missionary Society and the Society for the Propagation of the Gospel were very active. Sastriyar's background was in the Tamil Saiva tradition, though his father, after a few generations of Roman Catholicism, was converted to Protestantism. Krishnapillai, whose father was Vaishnava and mother Saiva, became a Protestant after a long struggle and resistance following the conversion of his brother.

Fewer than one-fourth of the more than a hundred literary pieces attributed to Sastriyar are printed. On the one hand, he denounces religions other than Christianity as false or inferior; on the other hand, he seems to be very liberal in adopting Hindu and Islamic terms to express devotion to Christ. He calls God Brahman with such adjectives as "gracious", "ancient", "supreme" and, in the style of Saiva and Vaishnava devotional literature, attributes to God such qualities as transcending religions and scriptures and having no bottom, top or middle, and such names as endless shepherd of eight qualities and six qualities, ancient one of Vedanta and supreme substance. He refers to the word of God in terms of *Tiruvacakam* and *Tirumantiram*, the famous Saiva devotional texts, and ascribes the truth of the four *Vedas* and *Sastras* to God.

Krishnapillai is equally polemical regarding other religions, but he demonstrates the other side as well. His *Ratchanya Yatrikam* ("Journey of Salvation") is based on John Bunyan's *Pilgrim's Progress* with a Tamil flavour. His epithets for God and Jesus exhibit a familiarity with Saiva and Vaishnava devotional texts. He compares the cross of Jesus to the thorny cart of a lover found in the Sankam literature. In what is now the first lyric in the authorized lyric book of the mainline churches, Krishnapillai incorporates ideas and phrases from the Hindu texts, calling God *Sat* ("reality"), *Cit* ("intelligence") and *Ananda* ("joy"), forming the Trinity. Elsewhere he refers to God as "Father, Mother and Friend". His prayer, "I do not cling to you, yet you do not give up your grasp of me", echoes the southern school of Vaishnavism, in which the operation of divine grace is portrayed in the image of a cat grasping a kitten.

Krishnapillai's other book *Ratchanya Camaya Nirnayam* ("Determination of the Religion of Salvation") was the first "systematic" study of other religions by a Christian Tamil. He gleans from the Hindu scriptures the qualities of the Supreme God and shows how these do not in fact characterize the gods and goddesses of the Hindu pantheon but are applicable to the God of the Bible.

One other noteworthy poet is Mayuram Vedanayakar (1826-1889), a friend of the poor and advocate of women's rights and women's education. Vedanayakar was a committed Catholic, but his inter-religious lyrics can be sung by all devotees of God regardless of their religious adherence. They describe God as supreme and universal, acknowledge human frailty and the human predicament, extol God's love and devotion and express ethical concerns, thus implying the need for inter-religious cooperation on behalf of social change, which is the need of the hour. Vedanayakar had close friends in both Hindu and Christian circles. Meenakshi Sundaram Pillai, a great Saivite Tamil scholar, was so fond of Vedanayagar that he composed a lengthy poem of 438 verses on him. At the same time, he maintained a close relationship with Christian poets like Krishnapillai.

Social reformers

A movement which shook the Tamil consciousness in this century and still remains popular was that started by Periyar E.V. Ramasamy (1879-1973). A rationalist, atheist and social reformer with a revolutionary vision, Ramasamy left the Congress Party for ideological reasons. After some time in the Justice Party and the Self-Respect Movement, he founded the Dravidian Movement and was an outspoken advocate of a separate land for the Dravidians.

Periyar was a strong opponent of religion and exposed the elements of Hindu mythology which served to legitimize brahminic oppression in every sphere of life. His opposition to other Indian religions was less thoroughgoing. According to a biographer,

> Periyar's criticism of Islam, Buddhism and Christianity comes out as opportune when serving his ideological propaganda, but contains little of deeper analysis. He can speak appreciatively of them when finding in them ethical principles of equality and justice, thus advocating them if they prove to be an alternative to Brahmanic Hinduism. As religions, however, they are hit by accusations of superstition, exploitation and irrationalism. These religions, in spite of their comparatively long presence in India, seem to have little part in forming, or breaking, the traditionally dominant Hindu Brahmin society, with the result that Periyar is obviously less concerned with them. [3]

Originally a follower of Periyar, C.N. Annadurai (1909-1969) left him in 1949 over disagreements on personal and ideological matters to found the DMK (Progressive Dravidian Federation). Annadurai was an eloquent speaker and prolific writer, some of whose short stories were staged in theatres or filmed. In 1967 he became the first chief minister of a non-Congress government in Madras, and it was he who was responsible for changing the name of Madras State to Tamilnadu.

Under the slogan "one God, one race", Annadurai emphasized the cultural identity of the Tamils. He became extremely popular and was universally known in Tamilnadu as Anna ("elder brother"). His funeral, viewed by nearly three million people, was the largest ever seen in the state:

> Twenty-eight mourners, riding on the roof of a packed train coming from the southern city of Madurai, were killed when

they were swept from the train roof by the iron girders of a bridge. Anna's body was covered both by the national tri-colour and by the red and black DMK flag. [4]

People of all walks of life come to visit his black marble tomb on the Marina Beach in Madras. An eternal flame burns next to it, and his well-known slogan — the Tamil words for Dignity, Duty and Discipline — is engraved on it.

Cinema and culture

Annadurai's 1949 film *Velaikari* ("The Servant Maiden"), a forthright exposé of the hypocrisy of religion and how the rich live off the sweat of the poor, is a vivid example of the influence of cinema on the development of Tamil culture. Some films have been particularly effective in conveying to the masses sharp criticisms of traditional notions perpetuated by religion and the structure of society. In so doing, one writer has said, these films

> have achieved what the feeble voice of the street preachers and evangelists of the Christian churches could not do by vehement vocal attacks on idol worship and its futility. These movies were seen and these challenging questions were heard by many people all over the state. In Trichy alone, a city in the southern part of the state, the film *Parasakti* was shown continuously for 35 weeks in just one theatre. That many days and nights people were challenged to do some self-searching regarding their worship of idols. [5]

Released in 1952, *Parasakti* ("The Supreme Power") is worth examining in greater detail because it touches certain fundamental aspects of Tamil culture and Hindu religion. [6] The film chronicles the story of a family in Tamilnadu. Three brothers migrate to Burma to seek work, while their only sister Kalyani stays at home and is married. One of the brothers plans to attend the wedding but is robbed on the way, and only reaches home much later after considerable hardship. When he arrives, he learns that his sister has been widowed. He takes a false name to suppress the shock he has undergone, but stays close to his sister to protect her.

Kalyani is committed to the Hindu ideals for widowhood and strives to keep herself untainted by the world around, but her life becomes a series of trials when a young man, a rich man and then a pious man all try to rape her. In her desperation she eventually throws her own child into the river and attempts to take her own life, at which point she is arrested.

In the ensuing encounter at the sanctuary between Kalyani's brother Gunasekaran and the Hindu priest, as well as in the trial scene which follows, the film caustically exposed the superficiality of religious belief, creating a stir throughout the state by posing questions no one had hitherto dared to ask publicly. For example, Kalyani challenges the guardians of the law of the state and the religious traditions:

> Do we belong to you or the state? Where did you go when my child and I were living on the street corner? What did you do when my child was sucking my dry breast in vain? Parvathy [the supreme goddess] did not come to feed my child as she did with St Navukkarasar [according to Hindu tradition].

Later, when Gunasekaran appears in court charged with causing turmoil in the temple and attempting to murder the priest, he thunders:

> Money chased my sister; she fled away. Luxury chased her; she was fleeing from its clutches. Piety chased my sister; she ran and ran and ran even to the very edges of her life. The state, which comes with law, should have stopped her and alleviated her problems. Did they do that? Did they let my sister live?

What Gunasekaran says in a dramatic scene in the sanctuary (where the priest has earlier tried to take advantage of Kalyani) cuts through to the hypocrisy and hollowness of the strictly vertical faith practised by many people. The priest, a guardian of a faith that looks towards God as Mother, has failed to see the worth of a woman: "Parasakti is mother to

34

you," Gunasekaran tells the priest. "Is my sister a prostitute for you?"

For the first time in Indian cinema, this film raised the issue impressed on ancient Israel by the prophets: "All who make idols are nothing and the things they delight in do not profit... And so they will be put to shame" (Isa. 44:9-20). Encountering the priest from behind the image of the goddess, Gunasekaran asks forthrightly: "When did Parasakti speak, O fool?" When the priest invokes the goddess for help, the brother shouts: "It is a stone; it won't speak... Your idols will not be able to help you. When you cry for help, let those idols of yours save you! A puff of wind will carry them off."

From the traditional long rhetorical speech by Gunasekaran in the courtroom scene which climaxes the film, it is clear that the target of criticism is not the religion itself, but the lack of depth in the religious system. In defending himself against the charges of disturbing the temple (which he has called "a den of robbers") and attempting to kill the priest, the hero says:

> I admit that I disturbed the temple worship. It was not because I did not like the temple but only because I did not want the temple to be used by evil-minded people... I attacked the priest not because he was pious but only because he was a hypocrite and a false religious leader.

A religious system which calls the goddess "our Mother" cannot be valid unless it also calls others "our sisters" and "our brothers".

The influence of cinema in Tamilnadu is extended by the popularity of the songs in the films. Hundreds of these are played over loudspeakers all over the cities, and are echoed in the humming and whistling of many people in whose memory they have become embedded. Those songs which denounce injustice, extol humanization or reflect on the contradictions and mystery of human life can have a considerable effect in stimulating people to think about the transformation of society.

Signs of renewal

It would be a mistake, however, to suppose on the basis of such critiques of religion that the whole of the Tamil Hindu tradition is outmoded and oppressive. There have also been remarkable moments of transcendence and change. For example, Ramalinga Swamy (1823-1874), also known as Vallalar, was a Saiva saint who culminated a line of Siddhas (wonder-workers and wandering poets) who had a very revolutionary outlook in the 19th century. Transcending Saivism, Vallalar spoke of a true path which is inter-religious and of a casteless and classless society. He described a religion of "inner light" which is also the light of knowledge, and formed an association which continues to propagate his ideas and ideals. [7]

In recent years folk traditions have been approached with fresh eyes, and the liberating potential beneath certain "ambiguous beliefs and practices" has been identified. On the basis of research in several Tamilnadu villages, my colleague J.T. Appavoo has pointed to the alternative media characteristics found in Tamil folklore, both in the area of corporate participation and skill training and in the realm of popular protest against the oppressive systems of caste and economic discrimination, evident in songs, legends and stories. [8]

Other research has revealed the unmatched sense of bonding in Hindu communities. For example, if there is a breach in the community, there is no worship in the temple or shrine and no festivals are celebrated until there is reconciliation. A fitting symbol of this community bonding is corporate cooking, in which there is equal sharing of all parts of the animal slaughtered — in contrast to the system in the marketplace, where only the wealthy have access to the choicest parts of the animal, leaving the rest for others who cannot afford the best. The greatest resource for sustaining life in the villages is community support at the time of crisis, though this is declining with increased migration to towns and cities.

Under the rubric of the complementarity of gospel and culture we may also mention the contributions several Tamil theologians have made to Indian Christian theology, based on the concepts of classical traditions, some new cults which combine tradition with concern for liberation, and certain local festivals and customs which Tamil Christians have adapted.

NOTES

[1] B. Ziegenbalg, *Genealogy of the South Indian Gods*, New Delhi, Unity Book Service, repr. 1984, p.22.

[2] *Ibid.*, p.14.

[3] Anita Diehl, *Periyar E.V. Ramasamy*, Bombay, B.I. Publications, 1978, pp.43f.

[4] Charles Ryerson, *Regionalism and Religion: The Tamil Renaissance and Popular Hinduism*, Madras, Christian Literature Society, 1988, pp.108f.

[5] C.R.W. David, *Cinema as Medium of Communication in Tamilnadu*, Madras, Christian Literature Society, 1983, pp.36f.

[6] This summary is based on David, *ibid.*, pp.34-37.

[7] On Vallalar see further T. Dayanandan Francis, *The Mission and Message of Ramalinga Swamy*, Delhi, Motilal Banarsidas, 1990.

[8] J.T. Appavoo, *Folklore for Change*, Madurai, TTS Publications, 1986.

5. Compromise

In nearly twenty years of experience in serious inter-religious encounters, the most typical response I have heard from Hindus to the question of religious pluralism is that "our ways are different, but the goal is the same". Essentially, it is said, Hinduism and Christianity both stand for well-being, love and equality, but evils like caste and dowry, which discriminate against people, are practised in both traditions.

One response to this version of the familiar Hindu slogan of "many ways to one spot" is that of Krishnapillai in *Ratcanya Camaya Nirnayam*. He argues that the Creator who has made the ways of birth and death, of hunger and eating and rest, and the body structure of the species to be the same everywhere cannot have created contradictory religions. To those who compare the variety of religions with the variety of foods, he retorts that not all foods have the same nutritional value. Just as there can be poisonous food, so too there can be harmful religions and sects. Adapting the Hindu slogan, he suggests that while there may indeed be many roads to a village, the only safe way to travel there is on the one royal highway. Objectively speaking, the only reasonable conclusion is that there is only one religion relevant for all and that all other religions were not created by God. For Krishnapillai, Christianity is that religion; and all others, particularly Indian religions, are risky and indeed poisonous.

The reality of compromise

But the situation is not in fact so simple. We must honestly face the painful reality that the gospel has often been understood and projected in ways that have deprived it of its sharpness and newness. In other words, it stands compromised with traditions and notions which not only cannot adequately express it but may even obscure it. This is evident both in the Tamil churches and in the daily life of Tamil Christians.

In contrast to the situation in northern India, where most Christians are Dalits, the majority of Tamil congregations have members from different caste groups. In their worship services, they affirm that they are all children of one God and therefore brothers and sisters. What they are far less ready for is to become brothers-in-law and sisters-in-law through marriages beyond the barriers of caste. Some Christian families would prefer that their son or daughter marry a Hindu of the same caste than a Christian from another. Of course, such "mixed marriages" across caste lines do take place, but the proportion of these among Christians is not greater than among other religious groups. In some church buildings and church cemeteries in Tamilnadu there are dividing lines or walls marking caste distinctions. In a few cases, there are two churches in the same place for two different caste groups.

It is understandable that the first missionaries, after a period of resistance to the caste structure, justified maintaining it within the church on the ground that this was a cultural factor which had nothing to do with religion. No doubt many sincerely believed that change would come in due course and feared that trying to introduce it at the beginning would only arrest the movement towards conversions. But for sensitive Christians who believe in the transforming power of the gospel, the persistence of the caste system in the Christian church is a matter of deep embarrassment.

Despite the missionaries' remarkable concerns about the liberation of women, as we saw earlier, it is still true to a considerable extent that women have a lower status in the Tamil churches. Women are numerically stronger in participation in worship and in service, but male domination in the administrative and leadership posts is glaring. Moreover, the persistence of the dowry system has deprived a number of Christian women of a happy married life. After a long struggle within the Church of South India, a few dioceses have ordained women as presbyters, while others remain hesitant; and the other churches have yet to begin a process of discussion of this issue.

Studies of the Hindu impact on Christianity[1] have tended not to recognize sufficiently how certain notions popular among Tamil Christians distort the core vision of the Bible. For example, fatalism is evident in subtle ways when people say that it is their *karma* — the accumulated effect of actions done in previous lives — that causes them to suffer; or when they interpret accidents and calamities that befall them as the will of God. For some Christians, all religious acts are aimed solely at gaining the favour of a God who dictates the course of events in their life.

Similarly, studies on the vocabulary used in the Tamil Christian community[2] have generally failed to point out how certain common terms may distort the essential Christian meaning. To take some examples:

1. *Tevan* is the term for "God" in the popular Tamil Bible. Although a few scholars would argue that it comes from the Sanskrit root *div*, which means "shining", its use is misleading in several respects. *Tevas* in the Vedas are celestial beings of varying status; and the Saiva and Vaishnava texts hardly ever use this term for the Absolute. *Tevan* is also the name of one of the caste groups in Tamilnadu. More significantly, the term *Tevan* allows for feminine and plural forms. Scholars like S. Kulendran of Jaffna have argued that this term entered the Bible under the influence of the Hindu scholars who assisted the early missionaries in translating the Bible. While the Dravidian movements have popularized the Tamil terms *Iraivan* and *Kadavul* for God, these have not yet found much place in Bible translations or liturgies of the church.

2. *Atma* ("soul") is another term popular among Tamil Christians. Its use leads to the notion of a dichotomy between body and soul, connected with a split between the "sacred" and the "secular". For evangelical groups, the watchword of "winning souls" appears to suggest a process of registering people for heaven. Even though the term is used in the New Testament as a result of the influence of the Hellenistic world, it is important to recover the original biblical vision of humans as unitary beings.

3. *Kovil* and *Alayam*, the Tamil words for temple, are also used for church buildings. The church building is thus identified with the temple of the Old Testament and as something comparable with Hindu temples. Forgotten in this is the sense of the church as the meeting place of the congregation and the symbol of the sacred unity of people.

4. Similarly, presbyters are addressed as *Iyers*, the term used for Brahmin priests of the Saiva tradition. Recently, a commission of the Church of South India suggested substituting terms meaning "servant" for presbyters and "chief servant" for church leaders. So far, however, this suggestion has been largely ignored, as it threatens the glamour and reverence attached to Christian ministers, many of whom are happy to identify themselves with the priests of the Old Testament.

Compromise in everyday life

Most Tamil Christians will take into account the Hindu division of days and times into auspicious and inauspicious when they schedule an event like a house-warming ceremony or a wedding. Some will make vows before shrines or with popular preachers promising to do something for them if they achieve what they want; and successful experiences of this type are often propagated as Christian "witness".

While the gospel guarantees fullness of life for all by overturning existing systems of discrimination and injustice, what has become known as the "prosperity gospel", proclaimed by fundamentalist preachers, has recently been attracting large crowds in many places in Tamilnadu. Their songs and sermons centre on the term "blessing", understood primarily as economic prosperity, accumulation of power and influence, and success in life. In addition to the complacent attitude this creates among the "blessed people", they are willing to do nearly anything for the preachers of this gospel of prosperity.

Recently a kind of populist ethos has swept through the prominent groups of the Dravidian movement, with government programmes offering all sorts of material goods. The charity of the rich is publicly praised, while nothing is said about the unjust systems and methods by which they have gained their wealth, which is the main source of income for these groups and parties. Tamil Christians have also caught something of this ethos, as can be seen in many of their charitable programmes and in their crowd-pulling rallies and conventions.

A simple piety and a simple ethics of doing good seem to undergird the religious life of most Tamil Christians. If one analyzes the lyrics and songs they sing, it is evident that gaining mercy and intimacy with God is a recurring theme. Radio sermons and published devotions repeatedly urge listeners and readers to do good in order to enjoy life and please God and to avoid evil in order to escape suffering and damnation.

At the same time, the mood at the services of eucharist is funereal. Most Tamil Christians do not regard worship as a corporate celebration of life and faith in response to what God has done. Nor is eucharist seen as an open table at which the liberating work of God and Jesus' fellowship at table with sinners are remembered, the messianic feast realized and the commitment of God's people to the work of transformation renewed.

NOTES

[1] E.g. Gnana Robinson, ed., *The Influence of Hinduism on Christianity*, Madurai, TTS Publications, 1980.
[2] E.g. Bror Tiliander, *Christian and Hindu Terminology*, Uppsala, Almqvist and Wiksell, 1974.

6. Tensions and Temptations

The varying strategies of confrontation, complementarity and compromise reflect the reality that the encounter between gospel and culture is seldom an easy one. Tensions are inevitable. In this chapter we shall look briefly at some of the temptations that beset any effort to relate the two in the Tamil context.

Power struggles in the church

Studies on the relationship between people's movements and the expansion of Christianity show clearly that the conversion of most Tamil Christians by the missionaries was linked to the process of liberation from social oppression and economic backwardness. But even today, generations later, consciousness of the structures of society dominates all other dimensions for many Tamil Christians. One result of this is that Tamil churches are being torn apart by power struggles. Church leaders are often heard to complain that they have to spend so much of their time and energy on court cases that they have little time left over for study, reflection and prayer. Eyewitnesses have told of church council meetings at which 75 percent of the members were standing outside canvassing for elections while the worship service was going on inside. In some cases competition for power has degenerated into physical fighting.

Of course, it is not only Tamil churches that face this kind of struggle, and one can see evidence of this tendency already in the Bible. But what a significant witness could be provided in Tamilnadu if the church could offer a new way of administering power at a time when the state is undergoing a situation of turmoil because of conflicts over power! How can our affirmation of a servant-Lord and of the crucified power of God find concrete expression?

A characteristic tendency of minority churches is to preserve tradition and avoid change. The Tamil church is no exception. In view of this preference for the status quo in its own life, however, is its enthusiasm for converting Hindus and Muslims to Christianity not somewhat ironic?

Let me cite a specific example. A large congregation in Madurai supports five missionaries in the Cumbum Valley, about 100 kilometres from the city. The church is proud of these evangelists; and there is growing enthusiasm for increasing their number. However, at a meeting to which I was invited to review this mission work, the missionaries reported that they were having great difficulty converting people to Christianity, partly because Muslims and Hindus are also active in mission work there. In fact, the missionaries had no concrete cases of conversion to report. During the group prayer that followed, some participants were in tears, sorrowfully asking God why there were no conversions after they had spent so much money and sent five missionaries to the region.

I found the sincere concern expressed in these prayers moving. But several days later I was struck by a discussion that took place before the Sunday worship service in this same church. The guest minister that day had chosen two lyrics (indigenous Tamil music) and one hymn. But when the organist was given the numbers, he objected that the custom in that congregation for generations has been to sing two hymns and one lyric in the service. The pastor tried to persuade him that the numbers he had chosen were more appropriate for the sermon he would preach, but the objections only became stronger when other leaders of the congregation joined in — including a few who had prayed so movingly in the meeting some days earlier. What kind of attitude is it in which Christians are unable to move an inch while expecting Muslims and Hindus to undergo a conversion to Christianity that would involve miles of change for them?

Misplaced enthusiasm

A side effect of the Dravidian renaissance combined with modern technology is a virulent form of noise pollution as religious groups compete with each other in playing their devotional songs through loudspeakers. In Madurai the citizens' sleep may be disturbed at night by the prolonged noise from these loudspeakers, and dawn may be signalled by the most anarchic combination of "music" from different quarters.

In 1982 a conflict between Christians and Hindus in a place called Mondaicaud resulted in the destruction of hundreds of houses and the shooting and killing of six persons by the police. One of the terms of an initiative for peace and reconciliation by Kuntrakkudy Adigal, a Saiva social activist, was to bring down all the loudspeakers from church and temple towers, since this competitive amplification of religious songs had been one of the main sources of the conflict. Many Christian congregations were very reluctant to bring down the long horns and charged that the district administration was taking away the "life" of the churches there.

In any case, it was a matter of only a few weeks before loudspeaker horns began to reappear on the church towers, and songs and sermons were blasted with an increased volume. Some Hindu friends said in a discussion, "We do not enjoy your music very much. Why should we listen to your loud prayers, which are addressed to God? And your sermons address the congregation not in mild exhortations but with strong condemnations that have no relevance for us." They argued that the issue had nothing to do with faith, only with common sense. But such considerations have little effect on those who identify "Christian witness" with turning up the volume knob on an electronic amplifier and filling the walls of the church with Bible verses. So loudspeakers have continued to be the main cause of communal conflicts in that district.

Fundamentalism — in the sense of bearing false witness against neighbours of other faiths, a rigidly literalist approach to the Bible and verbal militancy — is an enemy of the gospel. It is tragic that fundamentalism has come to be equated with evangelism, but unfortunately all the enthusiasm for the faith and for the church seems to come from the fundamentalists. Little if any middle ground between fundamentalism and nominalism is apparent in the church.

Evangelistic enthusiasm, however, is not matched by an awareness of effective communication. Too often Christians seem to be answering questions which are not being asked, while the authentic questions raised in real life-situations remain unaddressed. Esoteric language, exaggeration and evaluation without empathy block communication of the gospel. A couple of anecdotes help to illustrate this problem. [1]

"Are you saved?", a Christian once asked a devout Hindu sitting next to him on a bus.

"What do you mean by that, brother?", came the reply.

"I am talking about being *saved*," the Christian responded. "Haven't you ever heard of that?"

Removing his spectacles and raising an eyebrow, the Hindu said politely, "Please speak slowly and clearly, so that I can follow your question."

Thinking that a good opportunity had been created to share the gospel, the Christian began to summarize the biblical story from the creation of the world to the coming of the Lord Jesus Christ to save sinners. But when he had finished, the face of the Hindu betrayed even greater confusion. With a deep sigh, the Christian said, "Perhaps you will not understand until I tell you my own story of salvation. You see, I was once a murderer, a smoker, a drunkard and sexually perverted. When I committed myself to Jesus, he at once saved me from these evils by washing me with his blood."

"I see," said the Hindu. "Now I understand. But, you see, by God's grace, I never was a murderer or a smoker or a drunkard or sexually perverted."

Taken aback, the Christian swallowed hard and said, with some embarrassment, "Oh, so you too speak of God's grace?"

"Certainly," said the Hindu. "Our poet-saints sing of 'Siva, the sea of grace'."

"But you worship many gods and goddesses as well as idols," said the Christian somewhat hesitantly.

The Hindu friend then raised his voice. "You are thoroughly mistaken. In fact, God is one. We call him Siva or Muruga; you call him Jesus; the Muslims worship him as Allah. Names or forms may be a thousand, but the reality is one."

Not knowing what further to say, the Christian turned helplessly to his friend sitting on his other side, who had earlier tried to discourage him from posing the question about salvation to the Hindu friend in the first place. This person, a student of theology who was oriented to inter-religious dialogue, persuaded him not to try to continue the conversation.

Another story happened on a bus travelling from Nager-coil to Thiruvananthapuram. As usual, the bus stopped at the beginning of a bridge near Martandam where there was a shrine. The passengers threw coins and firecrackers into the shrine before the bus moved on. A Christian preacher riding on the bus innocently asked the Hindu sitting next to him what the meaning of this act was. The Hindu explained that the deity of this shrine often went into deep meditation, forgetting the bridge and the world, and so it was necessary to wake him up.

When the Hindu learned in further conversation that the person who had asked him the question was a Christian minister, he added, "You see, only a few coins are necessary to wake up our deity, while you Christians spend thousands of rupees to wake up your deity by blasting your songs and prayers through loudspeakers!" The preacher had no response to make.

"Gospel and culture" was one of the themes discussed during the 1992 synod meeting of the Church of South India in Tirunelveli. The worship service on one day included the following prayer, attributed to the late D.T. Niles (1908-1970), the Tamil evangelical theologian from Sri Lanka who was a pioneer in both the Asian and worldwide ecumenical movement:

> O God, the parent of our Lord Jesus Christ and our Parent, You who are to us both Father and Mother, we who are your

children draw around your lotus feet to worship you. Your compassion is as the fragrance of the lotus. Though you are enthroned in the heavens, we may draw near to you, for your feet stand upon the earth where we humans dwell.

We see your compassion in Jesus. He gives content to the Hindu name for you — Siva, the Kindly One. He gives significance to the Muslim address of you — Allah, the Merciful. He embodies in the Godhead what the Buddhists worship in the Buddha — Compassion.

O God of all the universe, let our history teach us that we belong to you alone and that you belong to us. And you are sufficient, for in you we sinners find sonship and daughterhood again — the one thing that we most need.

A furor arose in the days and weeks that followed. There were protest meetings and protest leaflets, though few of those who were complaining had actually looked carefully at the content of the prayer. Fundamentalist magazines published alarmist articles about the "dangerous" direction in which the Church of South India was headed. Tamilnadu Theological Seminary came in for sharp attack, presumably because of its work in the use of Indian folk art, music and dance in Christian worship, though the seminary had nothing to do with this particular use of this particular prayer. I was one of those who wrote responses to the objections raised. While seeking to respect the sensibilities of the protestors and acknowledging their right not to join in the prayer during the worship, I reminded them of the earlier attempts at "inculturation" by Tamil Christian poets, whose lyrics they continue to sing. But the opponents of the prayer remained unconvinced.

The struggle to build community

Distinctive communities need recognition. But is it possible both to tend to their own identity and to see themselves as part of one humanity and one global community? Adding to the problem in Tamilnadu is the age-old oppression of certain communities and the public concessions granted to them in response.

Although the caste system is seen as oppressive, one wonders whether it is desirable to deprive people of their social cohesion, which is constituted by particular customs and manners. Even the Dalits, who are the worst victims of the caste system, seem to be happy in affirming their sub-caste identities. Christian Dalits, who do not receive concessions under current legislation, are no exception. This creates tensions within the church and at large. There is pressure within the church for campaigning to get the government to include Dalit Christians among the beneficiaries of concessions. Recently, there was a debate as to how long the government should continue to make these concessions. Some argued for continuing them indefinitely; others for a limited period; still others to modify them, retaining the reserved places for them in admission to academic institutions and employment but eliminating those who are economically well off from the list of beneficiaries. Predictably, that elicited an outcry from those who have long benefited from these "concessions".

Similar tensions are found in churches and Christian institutions. But one thing is clear. Unless the members of the Christian community transcend their particular identities and realize themselves as having been created as one human race and reconciled in one body by God through Jesus Christ (Eph. 2:16), the tension will continue and explode from time to time.

For many years a major element of the identity of the Christian community in Tamilnadu was its institutions for health and education, which also played a significant role in the propagation of the gospel; and many of these institutions continue to serve as centres of Christian service and symbols of Christian identity. But today government and other religious communities have similar institutions. At one time, if someone in Madurai spoke of the "mission hospital", it was assumed that the reference was to the Christian Mission Hospital. But now there is also a Meenakshi Mission Hospital, founded some five years ago and presently flourishing more than the Christian hospital. Moreover, institutions of the Ramakrishna Mission are already popular throughout Tamilnadu, while new missions, like the Vinayaka Mission, are beginning to grow.

In such a context should Christians continue to place the same emphasis on maintaining their institutions — particularly since the quality of service of many of them is declining as they function largely as battlefields for church politics? The only justification for continuing to maintain them would seem to be if their focus can be shifted in order to address contemporary problems more directly. For example, schools of general education might become centres of model education with vocational training and guidance counselling. Likewise, at least some of the general hospitals might be converted into healing centres specialized to serve, for example, alcoholics, psychiatric patients and persons living with AIDS — all of whose numbers are increasing daily in Tamilnadu. What is needed are leaders who are imaginative and courageous enough to break with the status quo.

We noted in an earlier chapter that the renaissance of the Tamil language and the Dravidian awakening have contributed to the selfhood and self-respect of the Tamils and the establishment of their separate identity. One area in which Dravidian movements have been vigilant is in combating the various efforts by the central government to impose the use of the north Indian language Hindi throughout the country. At the same time, the leaders of these movements seem to have no problem with English, which most of them speak fluently. Consequently, an artificial mixture has emerged, in which middle-class people seem to assume that combining Tamil and English in speech is a mark of being cultured. It is "fashionable" and "modern" to call the parents "Daddy" and "Mummy"; the traditional Tamil terms *Appa* and *Amma* are dismissed as unsophisticated.

Not without reason, Christians have been branded as culprits in this cultural artificiality, although there are some Christians among the Tamil scholars who are trying very hard to recover the proper use of Tamil in day-to-day life (with English of course free to remain as a language in its own right). Furthermore, Christians seem unable to jettison the so-called Christian Tamil developed by the early missionaries, which is virtually useless for communicating with a younger generation who read only modern Tamil. While the publication of a Common Tamil Bible by Catholics and Protestants is an ecumenical hallmark and could be an important contribution to resolving this problem, no one is optimistic that it will be easily accepted in many Protestant circles.

Populism, apathy and cooperation

Mass appeal was a speciality of the Dravidian movement. But one can raise pointed questions about the extent to which it in fact oriented the masses to a new vision of life and society. Or are they simply the victims of emotional manipulation? It is not uncommon to see people being hired and taken in trucks to attend political meetings and conferences. But if ideology and awareness are the monopoly of only a few leaders or a selected group, there will never be enough people who have the self-awareness, self-esteem and freedom of conscience to advance the interests of society as a whole.

Among those who are part of the political system, there is a clear tension between loyalty and criticism. The Tamilnadu political culture has no tolerance for criticism. Rebelliousness against a cabinet or party leader will be met with a violent reaction. Unfortunately, the church, which is supposed to witness to the gospel, is not much different. Yet if the right of criticism is not respected within the spectrum of a common commitment, the structure is bound to collapse some day.

Modernity, which alienates the poor, seems to have no shame about the contradictions that abound. Highly specialized doctors prescribe costly medicines for patients for whom it is a daily struggle just to survive. The religious centres at Cape Commorin, at the southern tip of Tamilnadu where the seas meet, attract millions of pilgrims from all over India. There is a thick jungle of luxury hotels. But if you walk outside, you will see people covering their faces with kerchiefs and closing their noses because of the foul-smelling open-air toilets. When a World Tamil Conference was held in Madurai several years ago, modern lavatories were built throughout the town. Today most of them are closed down and deserted, though the signboard "Modern Lavatory" is still posted. Similar standards of maintenance characterize everything from water taps on the streets to libraries in the universities. Meanwhile, the number of way-side shrines in the towns multiplies, with no one seeming to ask any questions about the need for them or their relevance.

We saw in Chapter 4 how cinema has been a powerful medium of communication for development and social trans-formation. While a few films continue to do what *Velaikari* and *Parasakti* did a generation ago, far more popular are those films which depict heroic violence in smashing the wicked and successful lovemaking in the midst of resistance and obstacles. At the same time, a cult is growing up around the most popular film stars. A few have even had shrines to them built by their fans. Many are openly acclaimed as "god of our heart". Heroes or heroines appearing on the screen are taken for real figures; and some actors have taken advantage of this phenomenon to begin new careers as successful politicians.

Tamils are generally noted for their tolerance. A good example is the city buses, overloaded with people packed inside and hanging on the outside. Yet the journey goes smoothly because everyone is willing to adjust to make a little bit of extra room for another passenger. But this same tolerance seems to be extended to injustice and corruption as well. People are used to travelling long distances to get a certificate or recommendation which could as easily be sent by post. Bureaucratic indifference is accepted, and people seem to have no trouble with offering bribes to persons ranging from lowly peons to high-ranking officers. Murmuring and lamentation about corruption usually conclude with the acknowledgment that "we can't do anything about it".

On the whole Tamils live in harmony with people of other faiths. However, in recent years there has been a growth of fanatic movements of Hindu revival trying to poison their minds. In this context, interfaith cooperation for social change is a crying need. Unilateral attempts in this area, even if they are genuine, will always arouse suspicion. For example, revivalist Hindus interpret action programmes of Christian groups as subtle ways of trying to convert Hindus. One is reminded of the story in the Acts of the Apostles about the exorcism performed by Paul and Silas on a slave girl. The owners dragged the apostles before the magistrate, complaining: "These men are disturbing our city; they are Jews and are advocating customs that are not lawful for us as Romans to adopt or observe" (Acts 16:20-21). Genuine liberation was labelled as cultural aggression.

But interfaith cooperation for social change has yet to take concrete shape in living situations. Simply inviting a few members from other religions to serve on the governing board of a programme is not enough. As far back as 1977 the Religious Friends Circle, a group of Hindus, Muslims and Christians meeting regularly under the auspices of Tamilnadu Theological Seminary, decided to start an inter-religious rehabilitation home for beggars suffering from leprosy in Madurai. But when the issue of financial support for such a project was raised, many stepped back. Today there is a greater interest in contributing small amounts to campaigns for peace-making and against violence. Again, initiatives taken by minorities often make the majority suspicious. It is the Hindu community in Tamilnadu which must initiate and work for radical changes, with the cooperation of the minorities. This is a point of common concern in the ongoing dialogue between different religious persons and groups.

7. Towards a Dialogical Openness

History may be seen as a series of experiments in human life in order to realize its fuller and finer dimensions. Developments in Tamil culture and the relationship of the gospel with certain aspects of it should be seen as part of these experiments. Experiments cannot be absolutized. There should be openness for new experiments and the courage to risk.

The People's Movement for the Reformation of the Church of South India (PMRCSI), founded in Madras in 1992, identified three major concerns: (1) a representative structure, including lay people at all levels but excluding employees of the institutions concerned; (2) a simple coordinating leadership, in which power will be limited and shared, including restructions on the term of office of leaders such as bishops; (3) development of a contextual, combative and comprehensive spirituality. The overall aim of this reformation is to recover the credibility of the church in Tamil soil and to realize the power of the gospel to exert a liberating influence on the society.

To focus the concern, power seems to be the fundamental factor to deal with. Despite extolling justice and love, Tamil traditions have not questioned power structures; and in the church the gospel has become enmeshed in power conflicts. Money power, muscle power and mass power are in the hands of a few who are able to exploit people by using these in subtle ways and shifting combinations. Both Christians and others need to take a good look once again at the story of the tree of the knowledge of good and evil planted in the Garden of Eden, which is a symbol of the limits on the human tendency to be all-knowing and all-powerful. The antidote to this tendency is the cross on which God "erased the record that stood against us with its legal demands. He set this aside, nailing it to the cross. He disarmed the rulers and authorities and made a public example of them, triumphing over them in it" (Col. 2:14f.). Jesus' death revealed the suffering love of God and his resurrection set a hope for humanity, for the love of God can be resisted, but it cannot be annihilated. Until all powers are brought to the feet of this crucified figure (1 Cor. 15:28), Jesus will rule projecting himself as a Lamb standing in the face of cruel beasts, having seven horns and seven eyes on the one hand and being slain on the other (Rev. 5:6).

Christians can realize the power of the gospel which gave them their present identity only by turning to this bipolar figure, attributing all power and authority to him and serving him with a crucified mind. Then only will they realize the critical relevance of the gospel for Tamil culture, confronting on certain fronts, complementing and being complemented on others, but never compromising with the controlling forces, no matter how glamorous and popular they may be.

After the death of C.N. Annadurai the Progressive Dravidian Federation (DMK) split into four parties. This fragmentation is likely to continue, not so much for ideological reasons as because of controversies over leadership. In any case, the result is a terrible weakening of the original force of this movement, opening the way for its earlier enemies to recoup their power under the same banner. The relevance of attributing all authority to a crucified figure and the need of developing a servant-style of leadership must be seen in the light of this reality.

The controlling forces that lead to undue competition have to be exposed in all the spheres of life. Literature, films and plays can simply serve to legitimize established patterns. But others can be entertaining, yet creative, enlightening and even challenging at the same time. A simple example comes from a mime performed by a group of five young girls. The starting point is the traditional game of "musical chairs". The five girls run around the four chairs until the music stops, when all rush to occupy the chairs. One is of course left out. After two more turns, two girls and one chair remain. But they are obviously good friends, and when the music stops neither wants to occupy the chair. Each one points her finger, asking the other to sit down. Finally, the two girls ask the girl left out on the last round to come and occupy the chair. She in turn points to the girl who was excluded before her, and so on. When all five are gathered around the one chair, the first to be left out comes up with a novel suggestion; and they all go together in search of a fifth chair, so that all of them will have a place to sit. The pointed message is that withdrawal from the competition and power struggles of those at the centre can lead to corporate solutions for common problems.

While talk of inculturation and a few practical attempts in this direction have been going on among a few Tamil Christian thinkers, strong voices have been raised recently for an authentic, creative and selective type of inculturation which keeps holistic liberation as its basis. Among these are T. Dayanandan Francis, who has reflected and written extensively on the Christian encounter with Tamil cultural traditions, both religious and secular. His studies on Tamil Saivism, Ramalinga Swamy and progressive secular thinkers have led him to extend a passionate call for Christians to take seriously the liberating potential of Tamil culture and to incorporate these into Christian theology and worship. As he says, "When there is snowfall in Rome, should Christians in Royapettah (Madras) hold an umbrella?" [1]

Ponnu Sathiasatchy, who has launched a programme on theological exploration of Tamil literature, calls for a radical reorientation and restructuring of the Tamil churches in the light of the transforming power of the gospel. For him, the search is not for new ways to plant the sapling of the gospel in Tamil soil but to identify similar or near-similar plants already growing in the Tamil garden.

As we have seen, Theophilus Appavoo and a few others have worked with Tamil folk traditions with a view to recapturing a counter-culture combined with the vision and values of the gospel which can frustrate the lopsided modernization which seems to suck the marrow out of Tamil bones.

Inculturation or indigenization has been a Christian concern since at least the beginning of this century. The ashram movement, Tamil forms of architecture, experiments in worship and the pioneering attempts at a Tamil Christian theology have been the expressions of this concern. For the most part, however, it seems that Christian Tamils tend to share the negative rather than positive cultural elements in their life. As the old proverb has it, they seem to strain at gnats while swallowing camels. Lighting an Indian lamp or chanting Indian music in a worship service is anathema to many. But they seem to have no difficulty with the caste system, dowry, the oppression of women, the abuse of children, hierarchical administrative structures.

Thus a church which seeks to be truly evangelical first needs a process of "deculturalization" of these negative elements before embarking upon a "reculturalization" which can incorporate whatever is good and liberating from the culture.

NOTE

[1] See my booklet, *Towards a Humanist Theology of Religious Harmony: Insights from the Writings of Dayanandan Francis*, Madras, Christian Literature Society, 1994.